Cosmopolitan Arts presents

Cosmopolitan City

A Youth Arts & Culture Project, supported by Children In Need

First published in Leicester, Great Britain in 2023 by
SanRoo Publishing

ISBN 978-1-8384077-5-9

Cover designed and interior setting by Jerusha Barnett-Cameron and Peril Design.

All Rights Reserved.
Copyright © Cosmopolitan Arts, 2023

The rights of each named author, and the designers of each piece of work, has been asserted by them in accordance with the Copyright, Designs and Patents Act 1988. No portion of this publication should be reproduced without the prior written permission of the respective creator.

No part of this publication may be reproduced, stored in a retrieval system or transmitted in any form, by any means, digital, electronic, photocopy, recorded or otherwise, without the prior written consent of the publisher, nor be otherwise circulated in any form by binding or cover other than that in which it is published without a similar condition including this condition being imposed on the subsequent purchaser.

Proudly published 2023 by

SanRoo Publishing
part of Inspiring You C.I.C
26 Bramble Way, Leicester, LE3 2GY, U.K.
www.sanroopublishing.co.uk

In Leicester town, not too far,

Many cultures from lands afar,

Come together, hand in hand,

At Cosmopolitan Arts, a camp so grand.

Jamaican, Antiguan, and Guyanese,

Faces from across the seas,

With so much diversity to behold,

A world of wonder, to unfold.

From Zimbabwe and The Gambia's vibrant beat,

Mawali and Tanzania's drumming feet,

Somalian, Nigerian, and Ghanaian flair,

Zambia's and Cameroon's culture and so many more all beyond compare.

From India and Pakistan too,

Many languages spoken, it's true,

A true melting pot, you'll find,

Different cultures, all intertwined.

So come and join us on this quest,

A place where every culture is blessed,

Together we'll learn and understand,

With love and kindness, hand in hand.

For in this world, we must embrace,

Every culture, every race,

Together we'll make the world right,

With understanding, love, and light.

CREDITS

Amanda Leandro - Project Manager + Producer

Marcus Joseph - Tutor + Group Editor

Words and pictures by the Cosmopolitan Arts Youth Group - Rahnell, Jezreel, Amaiya, Acacia, Samuel, Churno, Anam, Micheal, Tegwen, Tavian, Ayaat, Andile, Elle, Amarni, Brooke, L'uaeh, Lathun, Soleman, Remi, Nana, Elisha, Gabrielle, Celia, Celine, Roeshia, Celeste, Miami, Shay, Ava, Giovanni, Benjamin, Amy, Jude, Aleesha, Miriam, Isaiah.
(All names have been shortened for their protection.)

Setting by Jerusha Barnett-Cameron and Peril Design

ABOUT COSMOPOLITAN ARTS

Cosmopolitan Arts has delivered a series of youth arts projects from the African Caribbean Centre, Leicester, continuously over the past eight years, funded by Children In Need. Amanda and the team wish to thank them so much for their invaluable support.

Cosmopolitan Arts' work focuses on celebrating cultural diversity through the arts, to break down racial barriers and create better understanding. For this project, Cosmopolitan Arts Youth Group wrote a poem together and made illustrations to encapsulate their core values and highlight the magic of the work that we do together, to promote unity, integration and help make the world a better place to live.

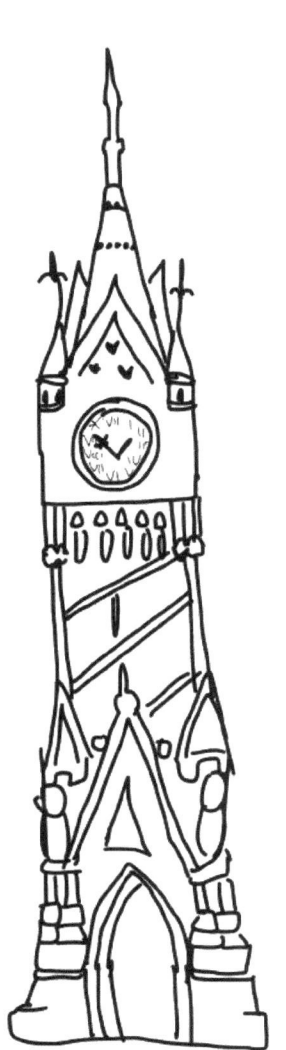

SanRoo Publishing

To find out more about SanRoo Publishing
visit our website at:

www.sanroopublishing.co.uk

Follow us on Facebook @SanRooPublishing

or on Twitter @SanRooWriters

SanRoo Publishing
is part of
Inspiring You C.I.C.

26 Bramble Way, Leicester, LE3 2GY
Registered Company No. : 1021381

www.ingramcontent.com/pod-product-compliance
Lightning Source LLC
Chambersburg PA
CBHW051332110526
44590CB00032B/4494